P9-DEM-824

A Note to Parents and Teachers

DK READERS is a compelling reading programme for children, designed in conjunction with leading literacy experts, including Linda B. Gambrell, Professor of Reading at Clemson University, Clemson, S.C. Dr. Gambrell has spent many years as a teacher and teacher educator specializing in literacy development. She has served as President of the National Reading Conference, College Reading Association, and will serve as President of the International Reading Association 2007–8.

Beautiful illustrations and superb full-color photographs combine with engaging, easy-to-read stories to offer a fresh approach to each subject in the series. Each DK READER is guaranteed to capture a child's interest while developing his or her reading skills, general knowledge, and love of reading.

The five levels of DK READERS are aimed at different reading abilities, enabling you to choose the books that are exactly right for your child:

Pre-level 1 – Learning to read
Level 1 – Beginning to read
Level 2 – Beginning to read alone
Level 3 – Reading alone
Level 4 – Proficient readers

The "normal" age at which a child begins to read can be anywhere from three to eight years old, so these levels are only a general guideline.

No matter which level you select, you can be sure that you are helping your child learn to read, then read to learn!

LONDON, NEW YORK, MUNICH,
MELBOURNE, AND DELHI

For Bookwork Ltd:
Senior Art Editor Kate Mullins
Author Annabel Blackledge

For Dorling Kindersley Ltd:
Brand Manager Lisa Lanzarini
Project Editor Lindsay Kent
Publishing Manager Simon Beecroft
Category Publisher Alex Allan
Production Rochelle Talary
DTP Designer Lauren Egan

Reading Consultant
Linda B. Gambrell

First American Edition, 2005

Published in the United States by
DK Publishing, Inc.
375 Hudson Street
New York, New York 10014

08 09   10 9 8 7 6 5 4 3

Copyright © 2005 Dorling Kindersley Limited

All images copyright © Dorling Kindersley
For further information see: www.dkimages.com

All rights reserved under International and Pan-American
Copyright Conventions. No part of this publication may
be reproduced, stored in a retrieval system, or transmitted
in any form or by any means, electronic, mechanical,
photocopying, recording or otherwise, without the prior
written permission of the copyright owner. Published in
Great Britain by Dorling Kindersley Limited.

A Cataloging-in-Publication record for this book
is available from the Library of Congress.

ISBN-13: 978-0-7566-1696-0 (pb)
ISBN-13: 978-0-7566-1695-3 (plc)

Reproduced by Media Development and Printing Ltd., UK
Printed and bound in China by L. Rex Printing Co. Ltd.

Discover more at
www.dk.com

READERS

I Want to Be a Ballerina

Written by Annabel Blackledge

DK

Today Jamie had
her first ballet lesson.

She put on her new
pink ballet shoes and
her new pink leotard.

She met a girl named Jennifer and
helped her with her ballet shoes.

shoes

Jamie's ballet teacher
is named Anna.
She is very good
at dancing.

Jamie met
the other children
in her class.

teacher

They were all excited
about learning to dance.

"First of all,
let's warm up our bodies,"
said Anna.

The children made spider shapes
with their hands.

Next, they pretended
to put on a crown.
They sat up straight and tall
like kings and queens.

Anna showed the class
how to stretch.

April pretended to be a tree
blowing in the wind.
First she stretched
to one side,
and then the other.

Jamie and Coco stretched their
legs by trying to touch their toes.

Anna taught the class
about ballet positions.
Jamie stood
with her heels together
and turned out her feet.
"That's called
first position,"
Anna told her.

2nd position

3rd position

1st position

barre

Then the children
stood at the barre (BAR).
They rose up on their toes.
They stood back on their heels.

"Try to keep your head up and
your back straight," said Anna.

Jamie tried to balance on tiptoe
without the barre.
It was hard
not to wobble!

tiptoe

The children pretended
to be flamingos.
They balanced on one leg and
spread their arms like wings.

Coco was very good at skipping. She showed the other children how to do it.

She kept her back straight and pointed her toes.

She skipped across the room with soft, light steps.

smile

Anna asked Jamie,
April, and Coco
to run across the room on tiptoe.
They tried to move
with soft, light steps.

"Don't forget to smile!"
called Anna.

Joe tried marching.
He swung his arms high.
He lifted his knees high and
pointed his toes.

Alex clapped
his hands and
Joe marched
to the beat.

clap

"Let's try some star jumps,"
said Anna.
"Who has lots of energy?"
"I do!" said Joe.

Joe pretended to be a rocket.
He curled up, then
shot into the air.
He made a star shape
by stretching out his arms and
his legs.

stretch

Next, the children made up their own dances to music.

Jamie pretended to be a leaf blowing around in the wind. They all tried to move softly like Anna had shown them.

Before the children
went home,
Anna let them
try on some costumes.

Jamie wore a skirt
made from lots
of layers of net.
It is called a tutu.

tutu

"In ballet, we say goodbye
with a curtsy (KURT-see),"
said Anna.
She showed Jamie how to curtsy.

Jamie crossed her feet
and bent her knees.
"Perfect!" said Anna.

"Thank you," said Jamie.
"I can't wait for
my next ballet lesson."

Picture word list

shoes

page 4

teacher

page 7

barre
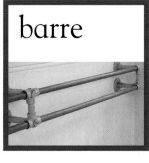
page 15

tiptoe
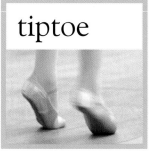
page 16

smile

page 20

clap

page 23

stretch

page 24

tutu

page 28